100 Sonn
of Galactic Love

Keith Hackwood

*for my wonderful
friend, Greg,
lets go love,

keith

18/10/04*

other books
by the same author

Charon's Hammer

100 Sonnets
of Galactic Love

KEITH HACKWOOD

PS AVALON
Glastonbury, England

First published in the U.K. in 2004 by PS Avalon

PS Avalon
Box 1865, Glastonbury
Somerset, BA6 8YR, U.K.

front & back cover photographs: Gareth Blayney
front cover illustration: Gareth Blayney

design: Will Parfitt

ISBN 0-9544764-4-1

CONTENTS

The Elemental Embrace

an introduction by
Mark Jones

One of the first things one might notice on approaching this volume is the sheer speed with which it was written: the first poem written on the 15th March 2002 and the one hundredth on the 21st of June the same year. If this is to be seen as more than mere haste or clumsiness on the part of the poet we might begin to understand the inspirational outpouring that found him literally unable to contain his effulgence- like the "raven in flight" as the act of naming is described in Sonnet III. Why this rush of verse, this black feathered song?

The poet, from the first stanza of the first sonnet makes it clear that Love is the reason why: "…a red star who even now is shining with effortless/ Magnificence across the pale mountains of my heart" - love of another who stands like a great luminary lighting the poet's way. This is the truth of the Other found in these poems, the interpenetration of meaning and life-force attained in truly opening to the divinity in another.

"What then, do we experience of thou?
- Just nothing. For we do not experience it.
What then do we know of thou?
- Just everything. For we know nothing isolated about it anymore."
I and Thou, Martin Buber.

Buber did not believe in the experience of divinity in another for to experience it would be to circumscribe the event that is the other's being and therefore reduce them to an 'it'. Instead, standing in the power of the Thou, this archetypal Other resounds eternally within the song of its creator and as a result we are never alone. In this manner the experience of being alive is both as a creator and as a part of the creation; in both we are realized.

In this collection of poems such participation mystique is evoked through love. In the combination of the creator and the created we have the perfect image for the evolution of the poet in this volume- for certainly the poet is the creator of the 100 Sonnets of Galactic Love - yet in making them he has been recreated, free of his own limitations and fear:

"If you keep ringing the bells how can I
Not hear you? The silence is bronzed by
Your summons, made special in the forge,

Of an endless call endlessly sparkling in the Listener."
Sonnet LXXXII

These poems have been created by the poet, by listening to the call of
the Other: the externalisation in form actually a response in innerness
to her endless blossoming, the writing an act of listening. In this
call and response, in this listening the clichés of cause and effect are
surprised and rudely awoken, the roles of actor and acted-upon, of
creator and creation are transposed, turned upside-down in order to
show that only in loving are we made alive enough to really be (and
therefore be able to love...):

"...The soft hands of
Compassion bow low to your emptiness, love, as in
Your stream I wash myself, standing naked, for the first time."
Sonnet LXXXVII

Through this love, soaked in the baptismal imagery of the Divine,
true Eros is liberated and we are able to witness the "coronation in
each Pan of the moist moment". Alchemical, Buddhist and Kabbalistic
imagery and associations are evoked by the poet to pay homage to
this coronation in the act of naming, an act which in Sonnet LXXXIV
comes "from the book of my Soul" and which in Sonnet XXXIV is a
peacock breaking its own heart to write 'I love you' on a stone. The
peacock here is rich with the symbolism of the Bodhisattva, the one
who makes the Mahayana Buddhist vow never to leave the world until
all have understood their liberation.

The poet explicitly yokes his Soul - his psychic life - to the poems,
echoing the original Adamic event - the first naming. In this context
he embodies words with meaning. This is no post-modern echo or
sojourn in the wasteland: love has healed the Fisher King and we are
allowed to dance in the play of meaning that words love to evoke.
Words themselves have become like the light refracted through a
prism, carriers of endless possibility and always with the hope of a
rainbow.

"The existence of I and the speaking of I are one and the same
thing. When a primary word is spoken the speaker enters the word and
takes his stand in it", says Buber clearly in meditation on the nature
of the word as God. In Kabbalistic thought a key primary idea or

archetypal model (platonic ideal) of the origins of humanity is Adam Kadmon an original or universal man from which all of humanity has emanated. In the Sonnets of Galactic Love through the poet's personal love of a woman, in his patience and dedication to truly seeing her and living in the knowledge of her (a divine event) the poet evokes an Eve Kadmon, the archetype of the original feminine. Once evoked the poet places himself through his blood-word on the altar of her being as it manifests itself in endless multiplicity throughout all of time and space.

In this way he attempts to live through patriarchy and its archaeologists "with their spades and tape measures" trying to quantify love (Sonnet II) in order to simply be the love. There is a radicalism in which love subverts the history the poet has known, our own alienated relationship to our time, and in which we return into an experience of the feminine mystery that like a burning star above his ship navigates him towards his home in the stars. In this way the sonnets are truly galactic:

> "I am the distance between night and day
> I am the colour of speed and silence
> I am on fire with hungry electric desire
>
> You are all the rainbows of summer
> All the living music of the sacred sun
> Redeemed, resolved in this nested surrender."
> *Sonnet C*

This is a feminine Logos. The Sun, traditionally the male aspect of the alchemical union (evoked by the poet in Sonnet X) is here shown as the true illumination of the feminine mystery and receptacle of the poet's desire. The image "You are all the rainbows of summer" is a wonderful example of the beauty evoked in these sonnets, the play on absence within presence and the presence found within the most subtle and empty of forms.

This is poetry that places itself firmly within the context of the great lyric tradition of European symbolism. I can hear the echoes of many voices, from Lorca and Rene Char to Blake and Yeats. A powerful influence is the enormous fertility and variety of Neruda's love poetry. More esoterically inheres the dark glitter of Paul Celan, not simply in the evocation of a woman's hair in her memory and presence but also in the way language is asked to turn double-faced to its own presence and absence. Rilke, in his Letters to a Young Poet, captures something of the heart of the personal and cosmic mission that Keith has set himself within these sonnets when he describes love as a

> "…high inducement to the individual to open, to become something in himself, to become world, to become world for himself for another's sake, it is a great exacting claim upon him, something that chooses him out and calls him to vast things."

I wonder if we as readers can follow the poet on such a journey? Can we receive the word as living witness to this love? For as Buber goes on to argue very convincingly in I and Thou such a love, rooted first in "mutual relation with a living centre" (of divinity) is the only source of true community, where we all might learn to live together in its knowledge. This is the true mutuality and interdependence that the poet realises in his love as he recognises in Sonnet LXIX that "we will climb ourselves up each other"; we might go even further and say that perhaps we all must do this if ever we are to make a marriage of self and other instead of dreaming our culture decadently on the edges of horrid collapse. Is Jacob's ladder a long, terrible, anguished and lonely climb into the ascending spheres? Or is it a shared play, a dance of two lovers heightened with every pass they make? Or could it even be the whole world, humankind climbing in vast chorus together? It is for each of us to answer these questions. I know which vision I prefer.

A close personal friend of the poet I feel proud to have been a witness to his journey and inspiration in writing these poems, proud to have seen someone I love articulate their inner music, proud to watch poetry valued highly and with such intent and proud to feel my own proximity to the evolution of a genuine and significant work of art that I believe has the power to change our lives. You will enjoy this collection.

Mark Jones
June 2004

Acknowledgements

The poet would like to acknowledge the support & friendship
of the following people in helping to bring
this project to fruition:

Diane, Mark (J), Will, Gareth, James,
Jon, Mark (K), Helen, David (B)

The Sonnets

Dedication

The One Hundred Sonnets of Galactic Love were written
between March-June 2002 as daily gifts from my re-awoken
'heart of genuine sadness' to my holy friend and inspirational
muse, Diane Segarra

Una a una
Alrededor de la luna,
Dos a dos
Alrededor del sol,
Y tres a tres
Para que los marfiles se duerman bien

('Vals en las ramas', Federico Garcia Lorca)

KH July 2004

I

The cold air chills its way through cotton, to make goose-bumps
    of my flesh
And remind me that winter remembers my name; and to sing
    like a shade
About the red star who even now is shining with effortless
Magnificence across the pale mountains of my heart.

'Bloodstorms and Eros!', the aurora borealis is holding our hands.
'Amor Y Alegria!' the fountainhead of dazzling life intones our
    sweat.
Under the never ending ocean of your presence a thousand million
Dolphins light the whale-path and sing their warm glitter forever.

O name of the unforgettable greenness of my seeing
Like the silver darkness of grace
Holding my hand and kissing me

In a royal explosion of sunlight, through pearlescent clouds,
Across the infinitude of ultimate darkness
To hold us to each other and to our Selves, his favourite twins.

15ᵗʰ March 2002

II

This morning the archaeologists came, with their spades and
Tape measures, investigating the parch-marks of my heart.
To dig and scrape for evidence of love's settlement,
And love I cannot now remember.

In black clay they found my teeth and bones, pottery shards
From my broken heart drew them deeper in.
The inspector found a ghost nail and dated it by tasting the
Dead iron, he knew how ordinary I had been.

But the digging made them deaf to the cheering wheat
Of the breeze, they did not hear the twilight head of Rumi
Posting letters to the Queen - 'the trees are Mary' he whispered,

And winked at you, I saw him do it;
Behind the back of science a different cat is licking her paws
And padding towards my passion to be stroked.

16ᵗʰ March 2002

III

Your naming was a raven, wheeling and healing in black
      and focused
Flight, over centuries of wet earth and the battlefields of men,
Initiating starlight into the mysteries of the black arrow,
Sweeping down funnels of space to the bare branch of the
moment.

I answered as a horse of purest white, cantering through the
      new season
With inquisitive ears, nostrils flared to the opened heart of
      the breeze.
I stepped and leapt among star-fires illumined by your bright
      darkness,
Fast sparks of flinty sky dashing from my magic shoes.

A raven, a horse, the royal procession of shade,
Under the ivy kindness of Bran and the silver
Moistness of words from ancient tongues.

Today I need no silicone, no circuits but these
Feathers, and the breath of beasts
On the threshold of turning the world.

17ᵗʰ March 2002

IV

I wrote your name in wet sand with a key held in my left hand,
The blue-red rock scree ahead, my simple eye between a low
Turbid tide and the promiseful horizon
Of the eastern shore, all pillowed under grey, grey skies.

Gulls attended my spellcasting with wistful shrieks and
Prophecies, the orange-beaked screeching of half-truths
half-secrets, as their feathered magic wings its way
On the white-capped breeze-torn sea.

'Diane' the sand replied, to my cuneiform invitation,
With supple, euphonious forms, conjuring blankets and
Warm hands, the sound of your tide undimmed

Your hair in the temple, in the street,
Upon numberless shorelines and shipwrecks
With the rush of new waves, and old mysteries.

17ᵗʰ March 2002

V

How should I try to count your hairs, which flow and whistle
From the aethyrs, always on fire with somnambulism?
I touched them once with the clay fingers of my heart
And all I have done since is cry.

What remedies can the mud provide to one with
A bare soul, one with more honey than a bear?
These tears are special envoys sent by the King of the World
To woo my celebration and sweeten winter's end.

Hair that flows in black nightingales of surrender,
In paradoxical centuries of
Silk, still broadcasting

Straight from the chorus of your lovely crown
To your ear upon my heart
Weaving patterns through its' bud.

18ᵗʰ March 2002

VI

Radiant days in the rivers of light, fluming through hopeful
Notes on the scale of initiation, yellow music from
The pulse of star-hearted grail seekers
Running and splashing our feet and our cheeks.

Or combing the decks of a pirate ship in search of a lost
Earring, a pearl of great price, a shining eye winking
Across the sail-torn shadow of night
And the ready conversation of the moon.

Your mouth invites passion with its fiery red hellos
Which fall like apples across the pitching deck
To roll and clasp at freedom

I saw you blow kisses at Saturn, who blushed and grew itchy
Knowing, as I do, that you are more than
Rainbows, more than salt-crystals, more than sleep.

19ᵗʰ March 2002

VII

Was there ever so much Beauty in the world?
Each day fields grow higher with their impossible
Wheat, cities shine like beacons to each other all
Through the annealing night -

Policemen wear designer boots and everywhere hopes
For the topaz delight of their master's law.
I saw a camel rehearsing, and a parrot with an eye-patch
Called out 'Verdad Y Justicia.'

Do not listen to them, love,
Do not heed their surfaces and science.
They are coming for us

But they cannot find us here
In the spiral arms of new galaxies of love,
Under the rich green blanket of the earth.

20th March 2002

VIII

I remember your hand in the clear waters of the stream
Among the glimmering crimson pebbles of desire,
Tickling the rainbow belly of the
Salmon of Wisdom.

For years you crouched and stroked there
With your eyes enraptured, your ears suffused
By the murmuring wonder of life,
You stirred and breathed and cried.

And now, in scales more mesmerising
Fresher than the melting snow,
You swim in every river

Flashing passion through a prism
Like silver arrows brilliantly
Murdering my fear.

20ᵗʰ March 2002

IX

This morning is a tightrope slung across the waterfall
Where tempests rear up and blossoms tumble like
Breadcrumbs on a platform, down into the
Precipitous arc of time.

I was late for the budding, a slow learner
Resisting wounds I knew to be mine,
Going deep into the manger of loss with my
Crushed grass pomade and my bruised pencil.

And now the day and night join hands and skip
With lusty dignity and sacramental grace
All along the ribbon of new wire

High above the rushing gorge, the rocks,
The foaming waters, caressed into
This elemental embrace.

21ˢᵗ March 2002

X

I give you blossoming Malkuth and Sol and Luna,
All the arrows of purification, quicksilver and quintessence
For your black hair and the whites of your eyes,
For the yellow puzzle in your heart's red whistling

Where the spinning essence laughs at the lies
The border guard is telling and swims through
The ribbons of Kether now becoming a golden ankh
Gliding through tearful waters, kissing the warm blue stones.

And I, in my Kairos, in
Saturn's melting lead, kneel and
Offer you my salty heart

As a badge of your completion,
As a shiny silver balloon to bounce
At the unnameable frenzy of G-d.

24th March 2002

XI

Where is the green lion going, following your star
Through long desert nights, praying by day
In the red dust, the sun's breath like fire
Between the singing hairs of his mane?

When will he choose the wisdom of the
Sand and wind, to be carried by surrender into
The arms of Hermaphroditus, to be stripped of his
Bandages, made holy for your touch?

The prince kneels, puts his head in the mouth of the king
Saying 'Father, let me feed you.
Let me be the medicine and bread.

Let the jewelled heart of my Beloved
Hold and stir us all the way
Past the last ships of breath.'

25th March 2002

XII

The snake was speaking Hebrew to the fountain
Calling on the rains to come and fill
The stone bowl with fish again,
For the tide has long since gone out

Long since left the sand to its own play.
I was sitting quietly, taking in the sunset
(which, on this occasion, spoke in broken Welsh
Recalling the spilled blood in the sky)

Wondering where a man can find wings
To take to the air and fly
Across each breath of distance

Between You and I,
Between a heart and a heartbeat,
With Quetzalcoatl my guide.

26th March 2002

XIII

I dance with my face always pointed to the East,
Like an archer seeking Good Friday,
Holding out against the flared pupils of age,
Firing blunt arrows at the rope-girl.

The seasons tease and smooth my cutlass,
Washing candles for Beethoven
In the black sea-swash of sounds,
A pair of the gulls shrieking on the waves.

'Let's swim from this tiny boat
That carries us on and on -
Let's plummet in our diamond skins

Down and down through the grieving
Sea, looking for the gravid moon
And her whispered, secret prayer'

27ʰ March 2002

XIV

Sweating moon is anxiously reciting the
Creed and the Manticore of Pauline spin,
Looking for a face to remember and befriend
In the lurid detumesence of belief;

She is wondering where she fits, after so long
Being ignored, being scapegoated and rammed,
Crucified and damned for her
Silver breast, her dream-fevered eye.

The scales of her division ring
Like bells across the hilltops
Splitting night in half

With the newest agony,
The five freshest wounds
Of the lunar blood.

28ᵗʰ March 2002
Maundy Thursday

XV

Once again, Love, the green has swept me up
And multiplied my passion
In plateaus, escarpments and folded rills
Moving like souls down Hay Bluff.

A lark saluted my tread
In holy elegies to the Sun
Your fingers curled round my own
When the freedom began

And transmitted your gleam
Like anvil sparks, like
Energy in endless expanses of motion,

Or the horse on the hill silhouetted,
Knowing that Christ, at Capel-Y-Ffin,
Held all the aces of the raven.

29th March 2002
Good Friday

XVI

Don't run away from the black earth, as it
Grinds and mashes itself awake,
Headings and navigation mean nothing
By this moment's chiaroscuro moth-wing.

Loams arise, and podsols, calling for the
Touch of many hands, desiring only
To be met, embraced, rejoiced in,
Like blueish silt kissing daimonic keels.

Wherever the peat memory exhales,
Another morning's flame
Crackles from its dark robe,

Singing inverted lullabies,
Sparkling new divinities across
The pantheon of our fear.

30ʰ March 2002

XVII

Approaching the house by the jasmine drive,
Fast by the yawning pomegranate gates
Just as evening sighs across in the
Unmistakeable softness of your footsteps,

We pause to salute the *penates* in their
Luggage introspection, and to bow our heads
To the *lares,* now gathered at the windows,
Offering distinction, like lime bodhisattvas.

How long since we lived here,
And felt the movement of seasons together
In the stonework of our own ageing.

How long it has been since
I saw you silhouetted by this moonstruck
Door, and leaned my ear to your dreaming.

31ˢᵗ March 2002
Easter Day

XVIII

I can take you where the way is forbidden -
Into the earth deeply, with only a heartbeat to light
Our ancient way. I hear the limestone song of
Our people, pouring like rain through Dan-Yr-Ogof.

Lobes of our remembering, huddling like nuns
Under showers in the nutritious dark - I hear the
Simple curtains draw grace around the marrow
Of this mineral pulse, this underworld of love.

Between the two waterfalls, in the ionised
Air's deep cleansing,
I know the gnomic process

Will reveal to me half an angel
If I whisper your name and bow before
The gentle elementals of this place.

1ˢᵗ April 2002

XIX

And you ranged in unseen, lemniscate, from out of the
Chartless reaches of deep space, spinning
Your alien webbing through the sentient heliopause,
Yellow eyes like seeds in a winnowing dance.

Past every majesty of solar hope, bare Neptune,
Pluto, Uranus and Saturn, Jupiter's fattened stare -
All the guardrooms of Mars, each missed your glowing
Heart, until you snuck behind the Moon

And whistled for attention down below;
On the blue mantle of Earth, my heart
Heard you calling in a voice I could not know,

Bringing remedies and poisons to this altar of
Love, grazing the ego-shields of men
With your searing, half-open lips.

2nd April 2002

XX

From your crown a cerise explosion throws its
Arms around the galaxy, in love with the milkshake
Trees of spring and the smelting of hearts in the
Butterfly furnace at the core of every star.

Your gravity entices me, shepherding my hermit
Thoughts, brings them to the folded feeling
Of the deepest dream, where star-children throw
Blossom across the universe in streaming beads,

And announce the age of freedom
In the flowing plasma heart-mind of the
Still unrequited G-d. In the parallax

Seduction of seven arrows, seven rays,
Seven new ways to kiss the speed
Of life, liquid diamonds echo blue fire.

3rd April 2002

XXI

Wet with the magic Fathers leave in their
Glistening Daughters' blood, to roar and revel
In passionate quest for the sublime
Cup, the supreme almond wand;

But snagged in marsh and boglands, where mud
Enveloped crocodiles rain coins at
A drear sky. Holding aloft a rusty sword,
When the Earth shakes You, Daughters, will

Be the first to know, in your blood,
In the blood of words intoned
Over violet fire and incense

Too sweet for mortal lungs. Like
Mapmakers your hands do magic
Creating the only star in sight.

4th April 2002

XXII

How many ways to offer up the swan feathers
Around my heart, clipped and quilled for dipping
In my blood? I scratch and trace the tails
Of words, rattling the emptiness like skeletons -

Reddening the page is the pelican's duty, and
No one knows the flashing prism's dance
But the peacock perched to whisper in your ear
Of fire and light and the journeying of the raven.

Sometimes I dream of the unicorn,
Galloping free through forests and valleys,
Sipping honey from streams

Which run down the centuries
Of your hair, spread down
To soothe the wounded earth.

5th April 2002

XXIII

You call to me along the canal, 'Come quickly'
In a voice as green as flowing life.
Compelled, I run to meet you, up the dusty towpath
Beside the turbid waters,

Not noticing the stones as they peek from
The mossy earth, or the still grey sluice
Where once the water overran to fill
The lost basin of time.

I see you under the giant oak, smiling,
As the ancient wizard turns his fingers
Into snakes and exploding buds,

And following the revolution of your
Gaze I see the sparkling dance of light
Across the holy water.

5ᵗʰ April 2002

XXIV

Outside the prison gates a sorrowing crowd
Is gathering, waiting for news of your arrest -
Seeking the fate that awaits the beautiful mirror
You gently sewed into the forehead of loss.

Doctors weep green tears and beg for forgiveness,
Lawyers, accountants and generals hang their heads
And mutter. A keening flower-girl scatters rosehips
And juniper under a column of rusting tanks.

The streets are quiet now,
Except for the pulse of fever
Coursing through the people.

In an upstairs window a gipsy
Girl tacks autumn leaves
To the genius branches of spring.

6th April 2002

XXV

Love became a drilling woodpecker
To hollow out my maple heart and
Let the syrup flow. My trunk peeled
In the sunlight among clouds of black bees.

Raining down on cherry blossoms, pink
And white, surfing a divine wind,
Magnificent Themis offered up laws
With which to stir the chaos of light

And shadow. Her budding lips
Announced a new age to the
Kosmos. My runny heart awoke

On the gossamer wings of
This butterfly, white against the
Green justice of your beauty.

7th April 2002

XXVI

The machine revered itself, becoming
Unrepentant and full up with its' own
Importance. Human eyes were loathed
For their umbilical gravitas and the ways

Of sleep and soul. No-one in the world
Bore a reflection anymore, not even the
President or his bankers, nor the freckled
Girl on the see-saw, her grazed knee on fire

With incomprehensible grief.
Then a spider spun its web
Across her face, like

A lover preying; like mummy-
Cloths and animations
In the name of some new healing.

8th April 2002

XXVII

Dawn's light is amplified by your kiss
Even at this hour, even as we wait for
The impact that will tell us what we
Cannot yet know. They put all their hopes in

Painting it white, this chunk of ancient
Intent now spiralling in it's cosmic dance
Towards our crown, our monarchy of love,
Coming to blacken our harness, to show us

How we straightened all the
Spirals of creation. They are
Sending for the scientists,

Measuring how long we have,
But your kiss swallows my
Fear like the sun drinks the night.

9ʰ April 2002

XXVIII

Sweetness unseen, but heard like
Soft sweeping fingers on a harp's
Strings, like the distant hint of lilac
Following the kindness of a star,

You reach me, you reach me.
All the chocolate of my world is
Melting now, the centuries slough
Like skin from a lizard, to dream me

Closer and still closer to
Your heart. Awash on spring
Tides of sensation, alive

In new geometries
Wild and simple, becoming
The spiral together.

9th April 2002

XXIX

Between the serried headstones of desire
The shaven sexton is digging a new hole,
Arching his back with each bite of the blade,
Each spadeful of red clay offered up to

The glimmering sky. The wind is picking
Blossoms from the cherry trees that line the
Path in pink and white arrays, falling like chosen
Snow onto his shoulders, into the warm earth.

This grave is fresh and ready
To receive my brokenness,
The declension of my root.

At the lych-gate of my heart your
Smile recites its prayers for the
Newly deceased and the nectar.

10th April 2002

XXX

As if the cosmic strings were dancing
Only for you, only for me, in their
Electroweak transition, their colour-blind
Forgiveness of each other's simple hands,

Gravity releases its secrets. Whispered
Across an aeon by the budding trees, the
Tireless ants and hummingbirds of light,
'Look at the stars! They are making love

Before our very eyes,
Inside our spaces and
Our loneliness, the stars!'

There is no end or promise,
No need, even for this
River of liquid suns.

11ᵗʰ April 2002

XXXI

Angel, I have heard you sing from the stone
Fountain in the centre of my soul, turning my
Ears to light, such fluidity and grace. Here
I am, in service to the children of your song.

Pan came first, from the wide spaces on
The wild green branch of life, with wondrous
Isis shining indestructibly,
Hovering in a dream of burnished gold

To dance in circles, awash with
Smoke, hand in hand with rainbowed
Chiron, my masterful guide.

Yesterday I was lower
Than a blade of grass – Now
I see that healing is alive.

12th April 2002

XXXII

I wandered all night like a hermit – fat with
The darkness of an egg, to the blazing snakes
Of the desert, where poor men go to cry –
Reading aloud from the Book of Longing.

My heart was a moth, it's beating, dusty
Wings kept repeating your name, though
The air was too cold for insects, and the grey
Streak of dawn spelled out my numberless *hiraeth.*

Then, from the direction of your blood,
As the moon collapsed into sin,
Came the passionate smell of bread

Rising in the ovens of your love.
And I pecked like a crazy sparrow for
The crumbs that would redeem me.

12ᵗʰ April 2002

XXXIII

You know that it's true – the universe pivots
Around this daisy. Each breath of wind is a
Wave of delight to scoop and share dazzling
Yellow and white. Legions of star-bees attend it's

Needs with careful awareness and love, being
Themselves fed by it's nodding, exalted in the
Fire at its heart. My skin is a mirror of flowers,
Your mouth is a soft palace of joy, a home in the

Nectar of being. These raindrops bring
Light as a gift, falling upwards through
Gravity's intelligence to celebrate

In full the new and ancient emptiness.
Go, tell all your friends, it *is* true.
This daisy dissolves me in you.

13th April 2002

XXXIV

I cannot blame the moon for my separation from
The sun – day and night are but shades of light.
My heart does not bleed though, sponge-like, it
Is soaked in the golden co-splendour of blood.

Seaweed adrift on the open ocean is a rudderless
Raft, good enough without anchors, moving away
From itself, forgetting its blindness on the rhythms of
The wave. Upon its mat, with wet and ugly feet, a peacock

Pecks at the shells of the dead, ingesting
The poisons that already slew so many,
Breaking its heart into iridescent feathers.

The flash of a sword through sunlight
Opens these images wide, to write 'I love
You' with a feather upon a stone.

14ᵗʰ April 2002

XXXV

I catch no fish with this ruined net, nor set
Traps for molluscs in the glutinous mud;
I am a mapmaker with no *terra incognita*,
An octopus gambling his hunger on redemption.

Wherever the wind goes I go the other way,
The dust storms hurt my wretched eyes and cause
Me nothing but mischief. This sand is the worst kind
Of machine, impotent and blindly unrelenting.

You stood there, arms outstretched
Like a crucified angel, puffing your cheeks
And whistling away my suspicious gut

With the fire of your melody, chanting
New unbelievably beautiful koans
To the dancing company of crabs.

15th April 2002

XXXVI

What kind of place is this, where the royal
Green of life is snared, spent and ruined on
The grey sexuality of the dead? Where turbid
Cavitation wrecks the noblest nature ten

Fathoms underneath the marvellous? I cried
Acorns from my severed eyes for too many
Winter mornings, my nose pressed hard against
Some glass heaven, hungry for hearsay and numbers.

Then, like a cloud erupting from emptiness
Your voice encompassed my drying wounds,
My scars danced to the concords of unison

On tiptoes in the infinite kosmic flux; harmony
Streamed like lightning, like blood, like wildness
And health as you sang my name from your star.

16th April 2002

XXXVII

Today doesn't have enough tears to
Circumnavigate my impatience with its
Broomstick, brushing away the fantasies and
Purple cobwebs, polishing stones with grey rain.

Today is my crippled prose in a metal flask,
Rattling its medicine all around the hillside.
My bundle is heavier than it was before sunrise,
The Fathers in their silent march have found me

Squatting beside this stagnant pond. Their
Words mean nothing to me, like the barking of dogs;
I have no pennies for their softness

No rusty breastplates to lend them.
I am threaded through the needle of your heart
Like red cotton. Pull tighter Love, pull on.

17th April 2002

XXXVIII

From behind the window leaps the ploughman
Shaping the soil for the seed he will sow,
Painting the green earth in brown lines;
Stirring the gulls, who do not forget.

There's a heron over Babylon, staring through
Surfaces with magickal eyes, like a blue bird of
Truthfulness. I can hear her whispering feathers -
Wingbeats chase gold patterns through old clouds.

But I know nothing of ripples,
Nothing about the ripening of time –
I am the fish-skinned Zapatista

Shrieking 'Tierra Y Libertad' from
The depths to attract your flashing beak,
To catch imagination in this aching moment.

18th April 2002

XXXIX

I put my tail into my mouth to taste the rubies
You placed there in a snowstorm of forgiveness.
They swim through the noose of my being like
Iridescent lassoes, rustling up the longhorn beasts

Now grazing the inner planes of ignorance. You come
Like a blizzard of star-fire, like a pyroclastic rush
Sensuality on fire, wave after wave of sweetened
Earth reconfiguring my coal-deep body.

From underneath the skein of your
Passion, combing the fronds of this
Shoreline for new cements and pearls,

My hand takes the hilt of a gleaming sword -
My thumb draws blood-red patterns down its blade,
Praising your heart in my quest for a name.

19th April 2002

XL

Last night I dreamed about the infant
Who lives in a wicker cage, carried along
By the Androgyne. I took her, this tiny gorilla,
And brought her to my broken-down room

Where she got big, grew bold, stayed in
And went out in the rhythms of my life.
She taught me telepathy and stillness -
The courageous drunkenness of her heart.

At the window, in an opium sunrise,
A shaven prince took the robes. We
Headed to the cliff-top to throw stones

Into the ocean, to find bright
Spears and pierce the salt air
With cries of delight at your kindness.

20th April 2002

XLI

You pass me a sliver of moon-cheese with your
Tongue, becoming electric nectar in the
Brightness of the congealed evening, all in the
Name of surrender. The plums of our madness

Are ripening, Love. Here in the bowl of Sundays
A grey priestess is giving herself to the wall,
Inviting its blankness with redemptive dance.
Yes, the mosquitoes are all stung out tonight -

Even the wasps leave us alone with our
Jazz swordplay, saving their fire for a different
Story, another moment arisen

From the mint's royal presses.
Let's spend our coins on nakedness,
On a sprig of blue stars in the obsidian mirror.

21ˢᵗ April 2002

XLII

Covered in scriptures, and the oil of scrapped engines
Tasting of mechanised piety and the brute stain of
Slavery, these days court silicone, uplifted and
Smeared with elementally numberless suffering –

Brothers! Sisters! Children of the sand! Come
And see the blood! Come and see the tar and feathers
Sticking to the groin of the world, her shame,
His misery, made music by the priest's rabid drum!

The blood! The blood! Wherein our movements drown
And all the simple star-light boils away to dust! Leave the
Cobalt mantra of your sleep to stand naked here

By this river of blood. See! My Love is picking apples
From the highest branch. Her silver crown is flecked with
Tears, like a butterfly drying her newborn wings in the sun.

21ˢᵗ April 2002

XLIII

Love, put your hand on mine, let's take this brush
And dip its thirsty bristles deep into the
Yellow moment. Let's paint pentagrams on the
Surface of the water in the pool between your heart and mine.

Love, put your lips on mine, let's kiss away all distance
With our conjoined will, dancing through
The yellow maypole ribbons of the moment,
Passing light through melting air, breath to breath.

For too long we have believed in time, passed
Equinoxes alone in minor chords. Love,
Hear your voice in my throat, let your golden blood flow

Through me, take my feathers in between your toes,
Holding my garlands close, like the yearning of silver
Tears upon the curve of your breast.

21ˢᵗ April 2002

XLIV

Living in the cold side of the fire, in a transparent
Box made of repressed nylon and beige imagination,
These worry beads don't help one bit;
I feel out of tune when the reed hums in the breeze

Alienated from all the green mucus of the water.
There are cranes and bricks and steel girders
Jutting from the pyramid of my mind, creaking towards
Demolition or the next new civil development.

Come and unplan me, Love. Love, come and throw bicycles
And lipstick into my hunger. Feed stale bread to my ducking
Heart until the evening ripens, like a Faustian pact;

Mephistopheles stalks off on tiptoes,
Too ashamed to murder one last moment under the spell
Of your cymbals, under the dissolution of my grasp.

22nd April 2002

XLV

Life shimmers round in the primaries
Like a seagull breaking the waves, orange bill flashing
Down into shoaling opalescent fish,
For the slicing pasadoble of the hunt.

The streets are ablaze with roses and flaming words pinned
To the bare chest of love. In every heart
A dragon screams with the last pangs of ecstasy
Waiting for the lance to shiver with release.

Who can speak the sacred words
To open the vault of secrets? Who has
Courage to swallow these liquids, this sword

With the hilt made of fishscales, the
Eyes of an artist, a twin, a pregnant Sisyphus?
The sphinx whispers riddles to entice you.

23rd April 2002

XLVI

Come and shout your name across this valley
So the people on the other side will know
That you are growing, that you have bright
Ears to hear about the stealthy ecstasy they whisper.

Come and dance on this pinhead, with the angels
I invited, busy in their weaving of the blue vortex
And the naked clouds. Come and join us as we point
And laugh at leaping fish, gargling with tennis balls

In up-all-night rivers. Look! A million roses float by
In an endless equation, mathematically plotting the
Graph of my melting heart! They are reddening

The ballast of life's hot air balloon, which rises
Up from the pit of my will, taking to the skies, buoyant,
Unafraid. From up here I can see your brilliance.

23rd April 2002

XLVII

I want to breathe in and feel the shining stripes
Of light swirl to the very corners of my lungs,
Racing one another to deliver their oxygen messages
To my hungry dustbowl; the air sings your presence.

I want to recognise your scent in the
Temperature of this jungle, yellow foliage bursting
And peeling through new dimensions of taste,
Defying the sky with immense umbrellas of luck.

A leopard whistled for my conference -
He winked and offered me a single hair
Softly stolen from your memory's head.

I refused his strapless mystery,
Preferring this vessel and its toil
To another transgression of your blood.

24th April 2002

XLVIII

Of course there were those who denied it,
Who said your love was a shadow cast by driftwood
On a long windy beach at midnight. They swelled as
The tides rolled, sneezing diseases like starfish in wet sand.

Wave after wave laughed kindly around them,
Swash and backswash, as galaxies of grains caught between
Your toes. But they were hardened and dry and knew better;
Their voices denounced the sun for its revolutionary peace.

I knelt in a rockpool to sip your salt waters,
To run my fingers through the moist fronds of life
Which danced to rhythms in the deeps of my soul.

Your waves broke over me in an unending overture,
Arc after arc of impossible light, made possible now
By your gift in the lapis lazuli moment.

24th April 2002

XLIX

I am the good morning of the wandering planets, in their
Draughty parabolas, leaping over balconies
To serenade new Juliets with the deepest blue
Anyone ever saw. I don't know what the Underworld

Is under, but like Orpheus at the earthquake
I am transported. I am under lucid orbits, through
The milky brotherhood of stars, the sorority of rays,
Looking for you, your trace, your wide wide justice.

The bankers chased me from the temple;
Black laughter as they hurled their tokens over my head,
Shrieking 'Debtor!' like epiphanic toads.

For I am indeed in debt; I owe my life, this new
Light and all the electrum of my heart
To your brightness, and your kiss.

25th April 2002

L

Lend me the petal of your heart, Love
That I might be free of these dead chains,
For you are the flowering key,
The magickal tang of freshly scented rain.

I offer you my tiny lightning and the vistas
Of becoming which I dance, as in a web,
Across the gulf of dawn, and the moon's white
Muscles, imagining a kiss.

Truthfulness tastes of ginger today,
And the wild garlic of our passion cannot
Be masked, or casually contained.

Come and stir the pot as it bubbles,
Let me spoon you rich juices from the fire,
Curling together in the branches of surrender.

26ᵗʰ April 2002

LI

Your laughing is like milk bubbling from a spring,
Breaking down fences with its plural streams and
Declaring rebellion in the poor red townships of my heart.
An echo never ends, but touches even the smallest pips

Of myth, the bone and blood born up from the dark earth.
Through your eyes I see the world shed magic tears,
Drying the grey rags of cynicism on prayer-filled poles and
Green dreams, becoming chocolate for the hungry.

'Ya Basta!' chirps the hummingbird, hovering
At my forehead – 'Approach the white throne with
Only your heart for a badge'. I step and struggle with

These aching limbs, this care-worn soul body, through
The cutting wires of fear, the thorns of abandonment,
            laughing
As I come to bathe in the moonlit kiss your shine
            showers down.

27th April 2002

LII

Two men sat by the choking stream telling lies
About a third, beating out the tune of their acid with bent
Hammers. I could see their lips move, and the pale language
Of death spill carelessly, like rotting pears, into the sad water.

A darkish moon wandered by, musing to itself about puns -
Your beauty and the ribaldry of skin. What pregnancy in
Time consists of nothing but mirrors? The moon knew
The answer to all riddles, but we, the people, have forgotten

How to listen. Now there are only fat priests of one
Colour or another, and uniforms and straightened lines,
Angles too sharp to welcome the roundness of a breast

Or the shape of an ancient tear. These things are whispered
In the cracks of evening, by shy tigers and flightless birds
As we sneak past the barbed wire bankrolls to nuzzle at
           your side.

27ᵗʰ April 2002

LIII

Get used to that sound – it's the sound of the wolf howling
For Ragnarok, the twice-tested hoofbeats on snow
Of our Enemy approaching. Something else; from the
Bright clouds massing, the white devil grooms his

Forked tongue:– which blue chamber spins with anti-venom?
Courage is more than the absence of fear. The moment
       throbs in
Four sacred directions, a rancorous *perestroika* fuels up
Thin money for the greedy shaven patriarch.

In the evening you sewed by firelight
With silver thread, and softly
Your hands midwifed this robe,

This soul-skin. When you took
The thimble from your finger a
Drop of blood-light flew into forever.

28ᵗʰ April 2002

LIV

What does that naked old man want, stumbling from
His cave mouth, like a drunk Tragedian or a salty sea-goer?
His eyes are pestles, you and I are mortar, ground like
The shells of blue eggs under the fleetness of a hare,

Ground together into one dust. On a far-away hillside
The Sun and Moon bathe together in a wooden tub,
Unashamed and bright eyed under the shelter of a star-filled
Ash tree. Somewhere a raven calls and an eagle rides the wind.

Smoke rises through the yellow-berried scrub,
Is it you or me that ignites?
Are these my hands or yours

That pluck the stars, peel back their skins,
Revealing the intricate, succulent fruits
Which spray their citrus savour on our many tongues?

28th April 2002

LV

If the world shakes off its tail, like a lizard in a trap
I will question each pebble in history's scree,
Following your slope up and down and through the
Hollow focus of dead time; I will find the atom-thin

Barraka, where to have known you is to flame on
Top of every candle-heart. Scales fall away in the
Syntax of spring, rooting like new exotic mint
Across light-years of longing, infinities in a teardrop

Of your light. The search is over before it begins,
Like ninenteen-seventy-six beyond pearl curtains
Or bubbling childhood brightly dancing for the

Numbers of enlightenment. The green lion rolls
Over on his back and heaves a huge moist sight,
Knowing once again the fullness of your will.

29th April 2002

LVI

In the smiling, leaping month of May
An ochre baritone will open wild raptures
From the horizon, summoning a coastline out
Of blue mist, upon which rest mermaids place their hearts.

Alabaster dragonflies chant plainsong from a lilac,
Relinquishing their fears in a spiral whirl,
Inviting us to join this ecstatic lyric dance.
All distances collapse, opening dimensions

Nameless and endless, stretched tight across the underside
Of leaky time, laughing as the space-waters flood in
And the vessel starts to sink.

'Launch the life boats!' Comes the cry,
And together we will leap, hand in hand
Into the floating garden of the heart.

30ᵗʰ April 2002

LVII

In the white room they are singing forever, your shade
       and mine.
In the morning their kisses rise like music skimming
       the coastline
Of desire; skin to skin they dance on newborn toes
And sing with cedarwood voices, calling each other home.

In the evening the box of secrets springs open and shines
       green
Like a breaking wave, humming Seven Sermons to the
       Dead through
Warm apple blankets. The midnight sun conspires to
       hide them
In the spaciousness of naked hopes and dreams.

In the white room they go on singing forever
Sky-dancing red clay and bone quadrilles,
Smiling like the guitar strings your fingers

Plucked that wine-rounded day. Those love-inspired
Trees, arms reaching up like cupbearers, to catch the pressings
Of your heart against my own in *Vinaros.*

7th May 2002

LVIII

Can you hear the bells, love? They are singing
Yellow sentences beneath the hum of crowds,
Like bronze whale-song underneath the scowl of engines,
Carrying my madness to the cliffs of your longing

On their gale-tossed sea; whispering in the tiny hours of
Dawn, of secret dakinis and olive flavoured stories from the
Deepest swell of soul. Out in the delta a heron stares at his own
Reflection and preens the blue feathers of his breast

Knowing that your gaze redeems him,
That your voice undoes him in the waters of
Marble surrender. Knowing that your flesh is

Made of glass-lightning flashing straight into
His gazing heart. Can you hear the bells, love,
As they chant for your passionate taste?

7ᵗʰ May 2002

LIX

Like two great silly dogs, loping through the mountains
On great thick paws, to play and ruff at the climbing sun -
Your heart outran mine, bounding from limestones crags,
Guardians of time's secret painting of the naked arrows

Unknown to all but those with animal noses. With great
Swigs of mountain air to cleanse and cool our burning throats,
Amid the scree and scrub glimmering in the afternoon sun, we
Stood and hoped underneath a Neolithic sky.

We stood and rooted our toes in the bronzed
Landscape's curves and rocky promontories,
Alchemically welded to the dream phoenix

Beyond the wind's coughing lens. Two suns set
In the mirror of your eyes, in the chasm between my
Need and this moment's helpless ignition.

8ᵗʰ May 2002

LX

Love, I can hear your breathing across the starfields
In between the pulsing glamour of materials and surfaces,
I can smell the tiniest wrinkle in your happiness falling
Like the wrong season's leaf, down and down into still water.

I don't want the stupid crown they gave me to blunder
Through your gentleness like an iron scorpion.
I don't want the furious history of my soul to thrust
Its spikenards and unspeakable lusts into your warm breast.

In my heat there rests a hummingbird, too tired to meet
The flower's nectar smile; his wingbeats fail at the vital
Moment, blown down by life's coruscating shadow.

Yet I would suck every venom from your flesh with my soft lips,
And drink the toxic attention like the very source of life,
Making colours in my rainbow tail, held aloft to offer you shade.

9th May 2002

LXI

In the open springtime of the light,
When stars flamed from vastness indivisible
From the whispers in your red flesh,
The scent of limes forgave us our pain.

The warm air hugged us lower and lower
Swimming through earth like the plough,
Mouths open in the angelic prayer of those
Who know their innocence is breaking apart.

Dry cracks split our souls like timber,
The resin of your freedom sings new ragas
To the sleepless creatures of the shore.

Nailed together in a clinker-built embrace
Each board of joy, each plank's sentient caress is
A vessel giving birth to love. Come, love, let us sail the skies.

9th May 2002

LXII

In the mother of the sun we shall find a witch hammered
Black by aeons of unlovely separation, her warped moss
Falls like hair across the shining brow of Apollo. Men
Feel for her breast in blind curiosity, women shun her

Scent, sensing degradation and all fear her coughing
Like the rattle of the serpent through the violet flame.
The sun remembers nothing of his history, nothing of
His nuclear rebirth, the incandescent miracle of form.

In the starry gaslight of new mysteries
The dead white moon swells and fades away
Like a pregnant ballerina on her pointed toes

Arms whirled out in moonbeams, reaching
Like a dervish, breathing deeply of the
Bloodstream welling up from far below.

10ᵗʰ May 2002

LXIII

Among the forests of priestly wood and stones
Piled up from fallen ziggurats long lost to dark roots
And flashing fixing minds, I creep like a Mayan fire
My skin gone blue and yellow with illiterate desires.

I peek into black wells and ancient stumps of trees, seeking out
The poorest soils, the driest dusty riverbeds and evenings
Where no flour has been milled from my heart. I step
Lightly across cold thorny paths, high into the thin air where

Breath is like a tight curl of smoke from a scroll,
The blood grows wilder in my veins, the music
Carves a new face in the stone surface of my hope.

Under every fallen leaf, behind the mountain snowline,
In the deep places and the hidden shells of temples long
                    forgotten,
In the forest and to the sea, I am looking for your slipper
                    made of tears.

10th May 2002

LXIV

The yellow petals rain from comets stripping
The sky of its panic, holding open the bloodshot
Jazz-wound of an eye, seeing more clearly now
How the paint has never dried on any cloud,

How the azure blues and Coptic greens of morning
Dance like Persian mystics across the slow horizon
Of humanity, spreading fragrant wishes in honour
Of insects and the despised. Strong music lets

The gritty daylight in with welcoming throat and
Effortless strides, like an opera made of giraffes
Or a father kneeling in the grapes of childhood.

Come under this awning, bright one, come into
The shade and be seen. The rhythm of your body is
An electric orange orbiting the thirst of my tongue.

11ᵗʰ May 2002

LXV

Sometimes the mind advances like a rash
Across the peninsula of an idea, drawing compulsive
Actions from the half-awake serpentine fire;
Itchiness covers the eyes of would-be seers with

Flakes and cones and rods of dissident will.
'What is?' you whisper, low and feral like
The bandit-hearted queen of these mysterious
Mountains, this shining sulphur sea.

I have no answer but the muscular imagination
That sold me to your covenant in compassionate
Aching, salubrious affection, the quilted ribs of

A black-and-amber bee, dipping his sting in the slow
Honey of your majestic wax, melting down towards
The light, felt only in cetacean echoes.

12ʰ May 2002

LXVI

Stretched through the cells of yesterday, without anchor
In the ocean of ticking isotopes or decaying static in
Between the meshed seconds, revolution spares the waves
The trouble of breaking. It is in the nature of emptiness to

Be empty, in the nature of the cobra to hiss; every god
Whose torso once shone with jewels and braided golden
Blood, now hums inorganic melodies through the cloudscape
Of our fractal sky. The earth once more breathes cold stone

From the ancient dampness. Do you remember the gorse
      of the dunes?
When the yellow flowers pushed their solos to the forefront
      of the moment,
And my heart fell away in rotten strips, burrowing through
      the dry earth?

In these scrubby hills of stone green dust, in the thin air
      of the chaparral
The sun calls its frozen energy into light, the oils of our
      bodies leap into bright
Vapour like eager genies, cusping the flux of ignition
      with invisible vivacity.

12ᵗʰ May 2002

LXVII

Secrets pour from the creamy elderflowers
Silent syrup from the womblight of Yesod
Called to this place by your glance
Through orchestral dream-fathoms and dance;

Shining from the wound on the tip of the branch
The glowing chant emerges and revolves,
Writing its name on the evening's chance,
Latent elves for the rhythmic vowels.

We can't contain such effervescent light,
Like extra-solar planets we wander the warm
Orbits of invisible distance

And swing between the heliopause of night
And the cascading melodies of other
Unknown bodies, kissing the dark edge bright.

13th May 2002

LXVIII

They use the shadow of numbers and straight lines,
This phrenology of surfaces, to perpetrate the
Theft of your *eidola* – stealing your reflection
From the mirror they held beneath my ghostly nose,

Then say that I am poking out my eyes when I sharpen my
Pencils with twisting vigour, they will say it in capitals;
No-one told the shark to bite, or the tiger to pad
Silently through the scrub – these animal professors

Consume the lonely data of dead white hands, roar
With the polymorphous symmetries of space, leap
Into the unknown void without valid insurance cover.

Passivity sucks at the teats of assent, the way of chains
Opens wider to swallow whole races, histories, economic
       miracles.
Love, come closer with your razor teeth, bite into my
       heart again.

14ᵗʰ May 2002

LXIX

Have you ever wondered about presence,
The Doppler-besotted media of a pale moon
Against lavender ropes? The ladder to the stars
Includes your rung, and the soles of my feet tread

Lightly towards your flexibility. Even now I
Am lying flat, braced with the brocades of a
Sentry, holding my breath for the step of your
Magic paws, inviting the jump-through-portal

Of your otherness. We will climb each other!
From the lowest crumbs beneath the floorboads
Of denial, we will climb Ourselves up each other!

Upon the porcelain fields, where witchcraft
Hums the themes of love, two new wanderers
Fascinate inky squid with their karate.

15th May 2002

LXX

Once I wanted to tell you about
Poppies blowing in the moody wind
In blood red fields, to sing you their
Luminous lullabies in rich overtones

Or bring you the sea in a saucer
And show you the swimming
Mermaids and their soporific waves,
Like diamond ripples in the light.

Now I can only speak simple words,
Fire and water and earth and air -
Dancing across the mystery of our

Strings like virtuouso bows,
Spitting with sparks of passion
For this love, this numberless reunion.

16th May 2002

LXXI

Theremin waves daub a petrol premonition
Through my aching mind, lapping at the
Business end of soulless grey apocalypse.
The greening of my magic will mean rude

Shifts, nomadic perils, all the sharp foliage
Of arrival. Underneath the gallows the weeds
Continue to climb, a barber gathers mandrakes
For his salad, clinking coins in a cloth hat.

Where are the patterns of nature?
The trees go nameless now, forgotten
Among kaleidoscopes of shimmering

Plastic surfaces. Your tears drip like justice
From your incorruptible eyes, solvent for the
Sinning skin I wear, in which I meet you, Love.

17th May 2002

LXXII

Sparrows nestle in the bars of windows
Sheltering from thunderous rain, wild
Sheets of darkness blown across the sky
Like black honey, squeezing out their sweetness

On all the petty jealousies below. I spied Martin
Heidegger pace his sour roundel, muttering
'This is the time of the double knot',
Looking for witches and struggle.

What neon sitar pressed the dome of Elvis
Under its kinky heel, and phased the gleaming
Pearl into foundling-houses, cities of light

Woven together in tapestries? And Love,
Your face becomes a pool of still water, your eyes
The freshest silence this world has ever known.

18th May 2002

LXXIII

So many pure things will happen through your smile
At the end of the day, happily sipping the wine of a
Wandering sun, calling for fresh summer poems
To decorate your wheat-fields and oceans; so

I become cylindrical, projecting my silver needs like
Torpedoes through the dull plumbing of established
Misery, coveting the U-Boat scenery of the professionally
Dead and their snow-filled pillowcases embroidered with lies.

The prince is out a'maying with his lady
And the green silken horses of the court
Hunting the unicorn one last time

Before the war machines
And the skies roll over and die.
The angels here have beards and breasts.

19ᵗʰ May 2002

LXXIV

The vilest misdemeanours bruise their
Filthy heads through denurturing tissue,
Despicable premonitions of a grey relation
Sold to the star-core magnet of the living flesh

By death pimps in stethoscope heaven, clutching
At hypodermic straws, licking the camel's music
On an iced-stick, dancing through colours of
Atomising hope. Take me out of me, beat this

Schizophrenia, this livid springtime dalek,
All along the night-time horizon, past Emmanuel
Swedenborg playing riffs on a little girl's kazoo,

Past the deadened heart, now tumbling through the
Aeon into dust, reverberating like balsamic vibhuti
That I will wear on my eye forever, crying out your name.

20th May 2002

LXXV

Here are the hug, the kiss and the Tree
The silvery tumble of leaves through streets
And the whistles of sparkling elders.
Here is the past of blood and stones

Of water and bones humming with magnetic
Healing, giving and taking the tides
Of sensation on journeys beyond Eros,
Beyond the river, the hillside, the thought-foam

Sea-dance of bottomless time in
History's flowing erosion,
The necessary stripe of a wound

Drawn across the furlongs of my heart,
Like your plough past midnight under
The moon's hips, gently rocking.

21ˢᵗ May 2002

LXXVI

Children playing in the drought
Forget their bruised knees, take
Leaps and giant skips at the sun,
Heads held high, casting no shadow

To stir the dense pharmacology of sight.
Seven stars perfected a grid to
Drool and delight in this mammal electricity,
The promised *tonglen* of excellent life

Striving for purpose and play,
Burrowing through lenses of gristle
To catch the wild feathers of simplicity

In luminous sculpted guitars.
Nowhere but here is the child fulfilled,
With every longing sigh of my wishbone.

22nd May 2002

LXXVII

Now that the chickens are born ready plucked
To please the single bulging eye of soulless
Men, be careful, love, in your gossamer dance
Thinning the very oxygen of this deep fire.

The beasts cry out in pain, humming new sophistries
Of the stomach, new semantics for our daily bread
Smearing gashed butter in crazy bladderwrack curtains
Stinking of dead semen and forgotten onyx lobes,

They are crying in their cells, weeping wild psychoses
Huddling into their introjects for a little peaceful wool,
A little broken promise to suck like a swollen thumb.

'The velvet is the skin' said the sapphire lioness, licking
The necks of her scruffy warm brood; I knew that her whispers
Were inviolable, like your knee in the grail of my open hand.

23rd May 2002

LXXVIII

Diving through the tenebrous depths
Past loafing planets and galactic yards
Where thoroughbread stars spit mutable
Acid across the deep universe, you swim

Down and down, seeking out pearls that
Spin and sparkle out of the limpid gloom,
Plucking cosmic petals from an ice rose
To wear in your hair, like delicate tears

Fomenting in a furious weeping of glad
Antinomian surrender, leaping like elastic
Mindstuff in the plasma-waltz of creation.

O Show me the wisdom of this phosphorous
Labyrinth, ride the yellow thought-dragons
Over my oyster-heart, to the lullaby of love.

24th May 2002

LXXIX

My dead son threw a rope for me into the second darkness
On the end of a saxophone's squeal, growling like
A lost tyre or a dog blinded by smoke and rain, hoping
That my poverty would re-embrace him in the

Rainbow-mother arms of Saturday's doll. But I had
No strength for courts or the imprint of heartbeats on
A sullen world; preferring the company of blackness
And donkeys, I stirred in the mezzanine dust for another

Child. And there I found her trace, like Utopia, like
Paleontology, like bruises on the sunset vinegar of the sky
To persuade and denounce me for this endless winding of

Hair, this fragile truth serum of dream pubesence, in a pulsing
Albedo kitchen, wherein the stink of poetry is forged and
Released in portions, each to the fittest secret of your glowing.

25th May 2002

LXXX

These days there are prayer-flags on the battlements
Risking their pennants in the high winds of change
Under scudding clouds and the dominatrix bowl of a blue
And lidless sky. There are priestesses doing cartwheels

Along the window-ledge of grey views, sticking to the walls
With lichens and mosses from between the skin's colander,
Blowing raspberry trumpets in mutable orbits around the sad
Chattels of wordless Jericho. I am troubled by an itch that

Sweetens and denies my breath through its fascination, its
Pollen-rusted schizophrenia, driving deeper down Babylon
                and up the
Pensioned column of my flesh, always percolating the stuck

Progressions of my heart's next chord, like serpentine
                perversity
Slithering to be fed at the whale-meat revolution of
                deep water,
Or the elegiac wave-crash of your mystery on a million
                joyous shores.

26ᵗʰ May 2002

LXXXI

Let your heart flow out like silk
Crossing the streams of this landscape
With impossible waves, in delicious epiphanies
More threads than a multicoloured boy emerge

And furnish the desert with spikes and glitter;
A silver girl presses peaches against the stone
Of her mouth, making new flour for your daily
Bread, reaching down into the oven of your cares

To knead and shape, to press out and mould
Each fibre of your love according to moonlight
And shy geometries. The play of these two is

Horsepower for the soul, talcum powder for the
Tired feet of the wanderer, witnessing the
Coronation in each Pan of the moist moment.

27th May 2002

LXXXII

If you keep ringing the bell, how can I
Not hear you? The silence is bronzed by
Your summons, made special in the forge
Of an endless call endlessly sparkling in the Listener.

I have paused from my task to hear the
Tongue of the invisible. I have stopped rubbing
Butter into the clouds to concentrate on
The whispers of the heart. Even the dogs

Are doing somersaults, eager for more.
Where did you find the golden tools
To unpick the heart and release its

Cavernous boom? Like the germs in
The raindrops, I am playing on a swing
And the sun is a smiling mirror-polished bell.

28th May 2002

LXXXIII

I've been up all night hunting down the comet
That best complements your eyes, singing about
The tenderness in your gaze until the planets got
Jealous and chased me away with rainbows;

And under a bush in my garden, in the spiderwebby
Palace of the insects, a galaxy of riotous life,
Even the slugs looked up from their leafy meal
To nod and bend their gluey horns under my words.

What is poetry then, if not your name
Spoken by glitter druids on love's throbbing solstice?
Where is Wednesday in this vast empty

Family of stars? Look up, O smiling flesh,
If up is over your head, and see the
Toddling wizards weave rays to honour your lips.

29ᵗʰ May 2002

LXXXIV

Who needs a guide to taste the warmth of the Sun
Or to know that it is the wind which runs its' fingers
Through your sensational hair? Did you expect the worst
Only to find that holiness drinks from the same cup

As the bitterest lips? Come along and watch the silks
Flying, gracefully undoing their whiteness in the
Moon's pool, where ribs and muscles and breath dance
Out of the dancers, to seduce our miserly hearts with

New and rotating bread. The planets line up together
And deliver their symmetrical promise,
All we have to do is listen with our flesh and be ready

For the call of the never-formed *chi*. Inside the
Book of my soul the ink grows amorous in
Its' rush to wet the tulips that flower in your eyes.

31ˢᵗ May 2002

LXXXV

'I am coming', said my shadow-twin, like
A ray of black-strobe difference swallowing the clouds
And sunset, 'I am coming to be with you and to hold
You in my arms once more, as all things pass away'.

A great screeching fills my heart with road-kill moments,
The crash of time against flesh, sand pours through the cracks
Of my heart, pours like flames, like jagged metal waves, like
The collapse of empires in calcining dust and invisible static;

Woman, where is the desperate compassion
That will slake my black and salty thirst and fill my heart
With apple-juice? How am I to know myself without

A mirror or a sister, the daimonic interference in the
Pattern of my acting? And will you press your luminous
Lips to this chipped vessel, and drink me in?

2nd June 2002

LXXXVI

When you are cotton you sigh like milk
In a golden cup, resting and waiting; and
When you are satin you roar like the sea
Across bold dimensions of passion, and lust

For freedom, for solitude, for the trombones of
Morning to ruffle your lustrous hair.
Inside your skin the beautiful moment grows,
Flowering into your cheeks and your red smile

Will you wear this leafy body in the vacuum
Of space, or take its buds and branches undersea?
Can each petal of your blossom breathe in

Timeless melody and send the missing colours
Back to me? I am rolling in the patterns of your garden,
With the basslines and the rhythms of adventure.

3rd June 2002

LXXXVII

Chiefs conspire to sweeten their losses
Rubbing limes into our eyes, squeezing faith
From the last few pips of decrepit law, kicking
The dust of today into the face of tomorrow

Like dogs in the heat, scraping for shade. But
Your freedom wears no metal crown, no stolen gems
Or mesmerising spectacle, your heartbeat invites the
Urban mystery to dance without once looking away.

I refuse the sponge soaked in sour tradition,
Doused with vain aspirations of stone thieves, all
Glued to this stick by grey adaptations of soul,

I will not suck from this desperation. The soft hands of
Compassion bow low to your emptiness, love, as in
Your stream I wash myself, standing naked for the first time.

4ᵗʰ June 2002

LXXXVIII

I lay down in the gutter near the station
With my head against a sack of rotting lusts,
And waited for your footsteps through the rain-soaked
Evening, answering the call of broken glass.

I have never been a shepherd, never caught a fish
Never even tried to scratch in the earth with these two hands,
I am not a skilful carver of wood or leather, I
Don't know how to find water in the dry times

Or anything about puppetry or grain. These keys are
Just bones, like my fingers. These words are just
Sobs that I could not keep in. I wanted you to be

The one who knew first and knew deepest that I am made
Of rice today. I am swollen with the tears of unborn men
And the moon lit a dark candle and walked away.

5th June 2002

LXXXIX

There is a river, Love, which flows from you
To me, I feel its singing waters draw
My heart's canoe towards the boiling rapids
Of your smile, where endless prayers of spray and

Semiotics dance from rock to rock, flashing
Free, expression-full, like notes from a wooden flute
In which my longing breath finds colour
In the holes your guiding heart has drilled.

This river grows like a tree, its branches flourish
Its trunk goes on deeper into the mild earth,
The fruit it bears in the autumn is the fruit of

Two hearts exploding, of star-birth, of
Traceries and unknown bodies enlightening the
Musk of sunset with new, unforgettable apples.

6ᵗʰ June 2002

XC

I thought I was drowning in the mud of
Age, a silted up river no longer navigable
By ships or desires of any size, all grey filth
And frozen ripples under the broken bridges

Of an old revolution. In that instant my kisses
Abolished books and words, came screaming from
The wastelands and hills holding flaming suns
In the mouths of their hunger, burning down

The libraries of self-interest, reclaiming
The waters for their own universal quench. They
Drew lots from a colourful psychic tree to see

Which one would find you, out there beyond the
Liberating sea, sailing your passionate galleon through
The curtains of emptiness and fragility.

7th June 2002

XCI

Time doesn't care that the orchids on my tongue
Will turn to ash under the longing breath of its kiss,
Bouncing through the walls of this clay fortress
Whispering rhymes and darkness, looking for the

Sharp incision of light. But I am tired of dryness,
I swarm with succulence and stopped-up lavas
Craning my paralysed neck against those shades
Who love things more than people.

Your scent is a veil of protection
Against the aristocratic horror of the image
Falling and falling like nails of rain

Or like broken stars in spinning fragments
Teasing the wound of the atmosphere
With flame-filled silencing fingers.

9ᵗʰ June 2002

XCII

I think that when the starfish closes her eyes
A dawn breaking symphony announces light
And liberty to each lonely crystal of the deep,
Every bud and dewdrop of particularity.

When Venus blows kisses through the lattice
Of evening's garden, and winks at the forlorn
Bucket of the moon, old jealousies flood the mantras
Of green and humming nature with petrol,

But when Monday curls its toes around the grey
Sponge of my lungs, caressing my sickness with needles,
Drilling orange filaments out of my bat-skin,

Your voice swims like a splinter of holy fire
To raze up this voodoo transcendence and
Swig from the coral-jar heart.

10ᵗʰ June 2002

XCIII

Often in our blindness we wage war
On the wrinkled edges of the heart
Telling ourselves we are hunting the unicorn
Or the fistful of enemy feathers;

Wise and idle parrot, what is it your cage
Lacks that you need to tease us this way
And that way, always eager for the opening
Into which so much purity can be hosed?

When I sit with my back against the
Blue skies of morning, or the blood red tusks
Of evening, sipping water from your

Tireless, cupped hands, Love, is it
Then that the berries make sense of me
And the chiascuro adventure begins?

11th June 2002

XCIV

There's a dancing cone of light behind your
Left shoulder, all blue and yellow in bands of
Rising magnetism and spin. You are quite unaware
Of this magic, feeling vulnerable and stretched

In the missing temple of your flesh, the dry cough
Of the word made dust. You cannot see the flames
That are pouring from your neck, cascading above your
Scalp like waterfalls of light, their fierceness doesn't

Hurt the spokes of healing. The earth breathes in alienation,
Breathes out the laser-thin focus of apples or intrigued cats,
Letting go of pain to wrestle with clouds or play in the

Blankets of night. I can see you burning, life on fire,
Transcending foliage and birdsong, released and sighing
In the silent blue physics of Love's ghost.

13th June 2002

XCV

These valiant horizons fulfil themselves in dissonance,
Registers of harmony in polymorphous dimensions,
Warp and weft, water and stone of the stomach of God.
Through a million grey lashes of time's wet belt

The clay reveals itself, comes to know the sibilant
Lie, its' enumerated homestead in the mind's tundra. Bones and
Lives snap and wriggle like worms in a terrible rain
Of mint, scalded by experience into new and poisonous forms.

The cats clear their throats, the lions hawk and spit.
In the halls of the soul's Abraxas
A dozen yellow fireworks are born and set upon

By feathered snakes, raising a chant to the mournful
Blood-red moon to free the carrion-witch
And the graceful Medusa inside.

14th June 2002

XCVI

Go! Run under the tongue of the livid river
Become scented with liquid mistakes and those
Casually gathered fungi, the toadstools of
Life's red breakfast, the sparkling little Pan

Of invisible mysteries unpicking the veins of
This terrible, holy despair. Rolling like rocks in
The water, gravid like a salmon for spawning, with
Grit and the stripes of Lent, the ripple of silence

Bubbling, like paper and tin beaten over an
Ancient wound, a sprig of timeless fear on
The stone bed of mortality, wet with murky light.

Darling, your fingers are bruised and cut by these
Sharp pebbles; come, let my mouth be your doctor,
Dance through the orphaned whirlpool of my love.

15th June 2002

XCVII

This is the glory of centaurs, both eyes fixed
Meanly on Saturn's cyclops, intending to milk the
Sky for meaning and gallop in feral orbits around
Your mad parade. Don't wait for feeling ready

Or the swollen belly of cheap mystique will swallow
Your ruin. Cough up the cynical lumps of dreaming
Wash the goat and the eagle in the same snowdrift, all
Of us rolling like drunken nuns through corridors of

Burnt sugar. Trees are falling, cities are cleft by concrete
Flames a thousand storeys high, the queen lies out in her sedan
Chair, fanning the fears of crusaders and chemists, blowing

Outremer kisses to lifeless generations of statues. There
In the evening's cracked basin, moth-soiled and rusted –
              are those
The wings of Lucifer? And are you whistling Greensleeves
              for my soul?

16th June 2002

XCVIII

Wherever you are, may your breath become joy and musk
And the forests welcome your footsteps through the rain
May your light be healing and clear at dusk
May saints from the country draw lots for your pain

May the planets unite in their choir
May any tears you cry sprout wings and rise
Into the leafy sky and continue higher
Until the mountains shake free from the fire

To brood and join instead in the voices
Of amber and fruit, the voices of gold and
Water, the rays of graceful sunlight

On the passion of a lake, a hymn to
Beauty, the justice of flowing angels,
May your love meet all of these, and smile.

18ᵗʰ June 2002

XCIX

I am a black pearl unnumbered by the sea
My gift was long since auctioned to the crabs
Whose claws stroke the flinty scarps of memory,
But the sun has not forgotten the taste of my blood

The moon doesn't refuse me when I remember
How to smile; the serpents treat me with venom, for
The nature of a snake is to slither, not to yawn
Through the boredom of soulless dolls.

Gardener, Book-keeper, servant of the living bees,
I am crowned when I turn my face to You,
I am raised and drowned in an avalanche, your presence.

Do not let me wander from your table, playing tag with ghosts,
May your astral nakedness be always my beacon
Be always my promise and my rootedness in You.

20th June 2002

C

In the longest light I will bend down to push aside
These jammed shutters, these veils of words between
Blood and soil; I will swim through earth and rock
Down to the mantle of molten love, the heart's boiling core.

And if the grieving lava should absolve me
If my fly-by-wire heart should remember being forged
I will recreate worlds, starfields, intricate beautiful mayhem
Eros obliterating ego-pastilles with I AM.

I am the distance between night and day
I am the colour of speed and silence
I am on fire with hungry electric desire

You are all the rainbows of summer
All the living music of the sacred sun
Redeemed, resolved in this nested surrender.

21ˢᵗ June 2002

Index of First Lines

 **PS AVALON PUBLISHING**

About PS Avalon

PS Avalon Publishing is an independent and committed publisher offering a complete publishing service, including editorial, manuscript preparation, printing, promotion, marketing and distribution. As a small publisher enabled to take full advantage of the latest technological advances, PS Avalon Publishing can offer an alternative route for aspiring authors working in our particular fields of interest.

As well as publishing, we offer a comprehensive education programme including courses, seminars, group retreats, and other opportunities for personal and spiritual growth. Whilst the nature of our work means we engage with people from all around the world, we are based in Glastonbury which is in the West Country of England.

new poetry books

Our purpose is to bring you the best new poetry with a psychospiritual content. Our intent is to make poetry relevant again, offering work that is contemplative and inspirational, with a dark, challenging edge.

self development books

We publish inspiring reading material aimed at enhancing your life development without overburdening you with too many words. Everything is kept as simple and as accessible as possible.

journals

With its full colour design, easy on-line availability, and most of all with its exciting and inspiring contents, *The Synthesist* journal is a popular offering to the psychospiritual world and beyond.

PS AVALON PUBLISHING
Box 1865, Glastonbury,
Somerset BA6 8YR, U.K.

www.psavalon.com

info@psavalon.com

Printed in the United Kingdom
by Lightning Source UK Ltd.
101917UKS00001B/169-288